How To R
Like A Pro

A Power-Packed Little Guide To Easily Read Tarot Cards

Katie Karma

Starlite Enterprises LLC

Table of Contents

SYNOPSIS

I bought my first tarot card deck in 1975 and began studying them using various books. They were complicated and confusing. In 1983, a woman read my cards, and I found her to be extremely accurate. She offered to teach me her methods. This book is actually comprised of the notes I received from her. I've been using these methods ever since.

Feel free to skip around in this book as it is not in any particular order! Learn what you need to learn.

Please remember that I'm not a professional writer, so forgive me for any grammatical errors, spelling mistakes, or typos!

Thanks,

Katie Karma

A FEW HINTS

If you are a beginner or early on in the learning process, I suggest that you use a simple deck. Of course, the Rider deck is the standard. My first deck was the Hoi Polloi. I still have that old worn-out deck, but I've added several other decks over the years. Hoi Polloi worked great since it was plainly stated on each card what the card was, like "Ace of Cups," "Three of Pentacles," and Ten of Wands," etc.

Always wrap your tarot cards in a cloth, preferably silk, but actually anything that is comprised of 100% will work. No blends should be used, like a polyester blend, something of that sort.

Remember to read your cards on some kind of fabric, like wood or cloth...no plastic or anything of that sort that is artificial. I used to read my cards all the time on my bed.

When starting to read, state "let me see what I see, say what I see, and remain free from karma." When done with your reading, clear the cards by stating "Let these cards be free of all energy that was infused in the reading and completely clear them of all karma."

These statements are not carved in stone. <u>You can come up with any statement you so desire to use.</u>

A FEW THOUGHTS

Tarot cards are tools. They bring out the subconscious mind of the querent or even you, if you are reading your own. You already know everything; you are just not *aware* of everything!

Yes, you *can* read your own cards although many "experts" will oppose that idea. This is my opinion; however, one time the cards let me know I would be meeting a new love when I was actually trying to determine which bar I would be working in. And yes... I met my future husband while I was tending bar a couple weeks later!

Newsflash...Tarot cards will *always* tell you what you *need* to know and not always necessarily what you *want* to know!

You will not find "reversed" meanings in this book. I look at reversed cards as only _delays_ and nothing else.

Now something you might have never heard... A seasoned reader doesn't even need to use the tarot cards. She (or he) can read the subconscious of the querent. Of course, one would have to have psychic ability to perform this feat! Many individuals have this ability, but most don't know how to develop it. Just remember we are all connected.

SPREADS AND METHODS

I'm aware of the fact that there are probably
hundreds of spreads, but some can be too darn
complicated. So, I suggest just using the Celtic
Cross, which consists of ten cards. One card in the
middle, one card to the right, then
counterclockwise to the top, and to the left, and to
the bottom, four cards to the right from bottom to
top, and lastly, one card on the middle card by
laying it lengthwise.

Newsflash: You can make up any darn spread you
desire. You can add more cards by going around
again and laying more cards up the side from
bottom to top. It's YOUR decision how YOU want
the spread to be. There are no rules, contrary to
what you might have read or been told in other
books. Use whatever spread feels good to YOU.
Of course, the cards should always be face up
when doing a spread!

Tarot cards are not meant to be read one at a time;
instead attempt to see them in groups. Naturally, it
depends on what cards are grouped together or in
close proximity.

4   The Emperor... is a person who gets what he asks for. He is wise with self-mastery and maintains stability in his life.

5   The Hierophant... is able to give guidance and is a teacher of the masses, one who takes everyone who comes for learning. This card represents high karma.

6   The Lovers... represent pure love and romance. Possibly a decision needs to be made for doing the best thing. Attitudes about love might have to be changed.

7   The Chariot... indicates triumph and victory. This person is reining over his or her own life and can be very successful if he or she chooses.

8   Strength... shows the ability to endure trouble until it turns into joy. It is the choice of the person to be strong, which will require a balance of power and decision making.

9   The Hermit... is alone and searching and an extreme loner. Very wise and has the ability to teach, although teaches only a chosen few, unlike the Hierophant.

10   Wheel of Fortune... is the highest card in the tarot as far as meaning is concerned. Represents extraordinary luck and good money or anything else that you want. This card instructs to not accept change, hold your ground, and stay in control. It can also indicate a sudden change of fortune, good or bad!

11   Justice... is a person who knows balance because they possess the insight and understanding to do so.

12   The Hanged Man... indicates a great deal of indecision and hanging in limbo instead. Suggests that the querent might have to give something up, but the querent is not sure if they want to do that. Doesn't want to let go of it, although it is most likely the best thing querent can do!

13   Death... contrary to possible belief, this card is good as it represents an emotional change or a death of an emotional situation and not physical death. Could indicate an end to a relationship or ending an involvement in an activity that is not beneficial to the querent.

14   Temperance... signifies a happy ending to trouble and indicates that the querent is in control of a situation. Represents a combination of all the right ingredients.

15   The Devil... warns you to be careful because something is being hidden, but this could be self-created bondage; can't or won't change mentally.

16   The Tower... indicates a sudden happening which querent weren't prepared for. It will be totally unexpected and will completely overturn querent's life with the ultimate result being independence from a negative situation.

17   The Star... indicates a welcoming inspiration which will produce some type of recognition. Also this is hinting that you need to always keep a resource of some type, which could be money or other resources, such as survival items.

18   The Moon... is a card of the subconscious indicating things we allow to fool us. Deceit and hidden enemies are indicated. The querent might be surprised since he or she is not seeing things right or the way they really are.

19   The Sun... reflects the physical body. It can be the giver or the taker of life. Watch for this card near health cards for it could be a warning or a suggestion; either happy times or pleasure in the simple life, or suggesting that the querent's lifestyle might be destroying his or her health.

20   Judgment... is the completion of the spiritual realm. The querent will come to believe in fate, that his or her day will come soon.

21 The World... is the card of material completion and success in whatever is attempted. Great card of wealth and riches; everything is good. The end of the journey of the cards that started with The Fool beginning his trip.

Note: Although the cards are numbered, I personally do not pay any attention to the numbers, only the meanings and surrounding cards!

THE MINOR ARCANA -- LITTLE CLUES

The following little hints are just clues on a given reading. Please never just see certain things for certain cards. Always see and say what you see!

ACES are beginnings, will, or force. ALWAYS the querent.

Ace of Cups... Marriage, one on one love, emotional state of mind, a possible beginning of a relationship.

Ace of Wands... New career, work and plans.

Ace of Pentacles... New money, raise in pay, more money in your hand.

Ace of Swords... Severing of a relationship depending on the cards around this card, it will determine if it is a friendship or romantic. This card can also indicate a surgery if around a health card, which would indicate what part of the body the surgery was going to be performed on.

TWOS are information; always two people involved.

Two of Cups... Indicates there is an understanding in love.

Two of Wands... Short journeys, going somewhere close by.

Two of Pentacles... Working out money problems.

Two of Swords... Going in too many different directions. Being in limbo and undecided.

THREES are communications, messages, good or bad news, and also brothers and sisters.

Three of Cups... A wedding or a reason to celebrate, including celebrating an engagement. Has to be a romantic celebration.

Three of Wands... A long journey for making a decision.

Three of Pentacles... Could be a marriage of money.

Three of Swords... A heartache, sorrow, and despair.

FOURS are foundations.

Four of Cups... An offer to return love (a lover trying to come back). The querent has the attitude that he or she can either take it or leave it.

Four of Wands... Buying a home or a home with a good foundation.

Four of Pentacles... A purchase of real estate or maybe an expense on a home. Could also be a Realtor.

Four of Swords... A funeral or sorrow in own home or an illness.

FIVES are worries and problems.

Five of Cups... A disappointment in love. Need to look ahead and not behind. Emotional negative thinking.

Five of Wands... A lot of hassles at work or with your plans.

Five of Pentacles... Worry about money, poverty mindset, scarcity mentality.

Five of Swords... Need to overcome your battles from within.

SIXES are responsibilities, employment, and health.

Six of Cups... Many friends and much company because of your adaptability with people. Reversed can mean loneliness and being homesick.

Six of Wands... Peace of mind at work or while doing your work at home.

Six of Pentacles... Balancing your budget and an even flow of money.

Six of Swords... A journey over or near water or a journey from within from troubled water to still water. A mental journey.

SEVENS are success and victory, more than enough, abundance.

Seven of Cups... A full heart in friends, love, material, and spirit.

Seven of Wands... Working out problems at work or with your work successfully.

Seven of Pentacles... Success with material gain.

Seven of Swords... Success over health problems. Could be a clue the querent might have a health worry (especially if this card is near any number five card)... or might be making plans for a checkup, either medical or dental, to continue good health.

EIGHTS are choice, luck, and balance...as above, so below. (Eight is the lucky number in China).

Eight of Cups... Death of a love, usually not a physical death but an emotional death.

Eight of Wands... Balanced day's work.

Eight of Pentacles... Independence in a self-supporting business; making more money than the querent has time to spend.

Eight of Swords... Self-inflicted boundaries, like being in a cage that is not locked.

NINES are inspirations or spirit.

Nine of Cups... The Wish card. Possibly a present from a loved one.

Nine of Wands... Tolerance of a job situation or any situation, getting ready for a change.

Nine of Pentacles... Expensive purchase, a car, home, enjoying wealth.

Nine of Swords... Worry that causes sickness, depression.

TENS are change and motion, like a wheel.

Ten of Cups... Total love and happiness.

Ten of Wands... Change of work or important plans for the better.

Ten of Pentacles... The wealth card, promise of wealth, a wealthy person.

Ten of Swords... An unjust situation from a lover or a friend. Wrongly treated for no reason.

THE FOUR ELEMENTS

The Cups are associated with water; hence the water signs of Cancer, Scorpio, and Pisces. They are involved with personal relationships and emotional situations.

The Pentacles are associated with earth; hence the earth signs of Taurus, Virgo, and Capricorn. They are involved with money, purchases, and material items.

The Swords are associated with air; hence the air signs of Gemini, Libra, and Aquarius. They are involved with difficulties, litigations, and mental health.

The Wands are associated with fire; hence the fire signs of Aries, Leo, and Sagittarius. They are involved with plans, work and travel.

THE COURT CARDS

King of Wands... Aries

Queen of Wands... Libra

Page of Wands... Sagittarius

King of Pentacles... Taurus

Queen of Pentacles... Virgo

Page of Pentacles... Capricorn

King of Swords... Gemini

Queen of Swords... Libra

Page of Swords... Aquarius

King of Cups... Cancer

Queen of Cups... Scorpio

Page of Cups... Pisces

The King of Wands (Aries) indicates an important job or plans

The King of Pentacles (Taurus) represents money and possessions

The King of Swords (Gemini) stands for authority and law

The King of Cups (Cancer) represents heavy emotions

The Queens of Wands (Leo) is fiery and authoritative

The Queen of Pentacles (Virgo) is wise with money and a saver

The Queen of Swords (Libra) is indecisive, has problem making a decision

The Queen of Cups (Scorpio) represents sex and passions

The Page of Wands (Sagittarius) is wise in work

The Page of Pentacles (Capricorn) has a small amount of money

The Page of Swords (Aquarius) will be unconventional

The Page of Cups (Pisces) is emotional and young-thinking

Knights are people thinking about the person or querent. They represent messengers and messages and will be received according to the suite showing.

If the Knight of Cups is showing _facing_ the querent, then the message will be expected the NEXT water sign period. If it is June, for example, the message will arrive in July.

IF the card is facing AWAY from the querent, then skip to the next water sign; the message will then arrive in November!

You always have to remember the sign the sun is in when you are doing a reading, so you can determine the timeframe quickly.

NOTE: I've found it to be much easier to just know what the current element is, whether it's fire, air, earth, or water. If you are unfamiliar with

what element rules which sign, refer to "The Four
Elements" chapter in this book. (Page 20)

HELPFUL LITTLE NOTES

Any two cards that appear to be male or female with no more than one card between them is a relationship.

LOVE AFFAIRS:

6 of Cups... Having affairs

7 of Swords... Flirt, tease, one-night stand

2 of Cups... Understanding already that it is an affair

1 of Cups... Beginning of a love affair

Moon... Breaking up of a love affair

Lovers... A boyfriend or girlfriend or someone that you are living with

DIVORCE:

Tower... Unexpected

1 of Swords... Severing a relationship

Death... Emotional death

MARRIAGE:

4 of Wands... Good home, good foundation

Lovers... Could be love at first sight

3 of Pentacles... Money involved in the union

The Empress... Indicates an engagement

10 of Cups... Happy family

9 of Cups... Whomever you are wishing for will come to fruition

BABY:

1 of Cups... Maybe not married

The Sun... New Life

The Tower... Unexpected

Death... Change emotionally

6 of Cups... Will bring querent pleasure

2 of Cups... Querent learning from her doctor that she is pregnant

GIFTS:

9 of Cups... Wish will come true (The Wish Card)

Sun... Happy gift (gift will make someone happy)

Empress... Possibly concerning a wedding or shower gift

4 of Cups... Someone will offer to give a gift, will take it or leave it

MAKING A VERY LARGE PURCHASE:

8 of Pentacles... Independently working for it

7 of Pentacles... Successful in obtaining the purchase

4 of Pentacles... Buying a house

9 of Pentacles... Purchasing a new car

10 of Pentacles... The wealth card

TRIP:

6 of Swords... A mental journey, meditation

2 of Wands... A short journey, maybe just running errands

3 of Wands... A longer journey, maybe to make a decision

(Wands mean travel along with plans)

NEW JOB:

The World... Always a new job or a new position

1 of Pentacles... A raise or promotion, more money in your hand

If in a spread there is the person (querent), knight, and the world, you know for sure that the person is getting or has started a new job

GROUPS OF CARDS

After a reading, take the cards that were used in the spread and separate them. Gather the Major Arcana cards and put them aside.

NOTE: If more than half of the total cards in the spread are Major Arcana cards, this indicates that the querent has major "challenges."

Group together the Court Cards and the Minor Arcana numbered cards and use the following list for more "clues."

4 Kings... Meetings with important people

3 Kings... High status, a prize, an honor, winning, help from important people

4 Queens... Many arguments and disagreements

3 Queens... Deception by a woman or women, gossip

4 Knights... Swiftness and urgency in messages and news

3 Knights... Unexpected encounters, swift news, surprises

4 Pages... New plans, new ideas, young people

3 Pages... The company of young people, thinking young, not grown up

4 Tens... Heavy responsibility and much anxiety, changes and motion

3 Tens... Commercial transactions, buying and selling

4 Nines... An extra burden of responsibility becomes an inspiration

3 Nines... Letters, messages, correspondence, spiritual

4 Eights... A torrent of news and information, balance and choice of learning

3 Eights... Much traveling, bustling to and fro, busy by choice

4 Sevens... Disappointment, especially in matters of love

3 Sevens... Agreements, contracts, alliances, successful meetings

4 Sixes... Pleasure from responsibilities, employment, good health

3 Sixes... Gain from responsibilities, employment, or health

4 Fives... Too many worries, possible problems concerning the heart

3 Fives... Disputes, disagreements, quarrels

4 Fours... Peace and quiet, rest

3 Fours... Hard work and ambition to attain a stronger foundation

4 Threes... Decisions, resolutions, communications

3 Threes... Deceit, gossip

4 Twos... Conversations, conferences, going in many different directions

3 Twos... Reorganization

4 Aces... A good sign, strong forces at work, starts

3 Aces... Money, success, new beginnings

NUMEROLOGY MADE SIMPLE

1: Beginnings

2: Information

3: Activities, Travel

4: Foundation, Home

5: Worries, Past

6: Responsibilities

7: Success

8: Balance, Power

9: Inspiration

10: Change and Motion

ASTROLOGICAL TRAITS

Aries... Self-starter; impulsive; has to be first; independent; pioneering; impatient; ambitious; aggressive; courageous; fiery; leader
Fire=Wands

Taurus... Stubborn; possessive; seeks material security; determined; stable; patient; loves food; cautious; conservative; dependable; practical
Earth=Pentacles

Gemini... Versatile; restless; sociable; needs freedom; curious; hard to concentrate on one thing; person; or idea; communicator; doubtful; needs to learn to relax; intellectual **Air=Swords**

Cancer... Moody; domestic; strong nurturing quality; active imagination; sensitive to environment; cautious; receptive; tenacious; intuitive; emotional **Water=Cups**

Leo... Generous; dramatic; passionate; personal magnetism; powerful; enthusiastic; proud; strong; independent; needs and gets recognition; fiery **Fire=Wands**

Virgo... Efficient; analytical; critical; values work; seeks perfection; wants results; wants to be of service; concerned with details, skeptical; admires accomplishments **Earth=Pentacles**

Libra... Diplomatic; sociable; seeks the balance; needs and promotes harmony; idealistic; charming; doesn't like to do things alone; just; indecisive **Air=Swords**

Scorpio... Intense nature; passionate; mysterious; shrewd; calculating; secretive; loner; resourceful; powerful; hides feelings; personal magnetism **Water=Cups**

Sagittarius... Optimistic; frank; honest; idealistic; needs freedom; seeks and speaks the truth;

enthusiastic; expansive; straightforward; explores **Fire=Wands**

Capricorn...Serious, old ways; cautious; disciplined; conservative; hard worker; seeks financial and professional security; dependable; economical; conscientious **Earth=Pentacles**

Aquarius... Unconventional; friends are important; lives in future; demands freedom; detached; impersonal; humanitarian; original; group activity; unique **Air=Swords**

Pisces... Psychic; compassionate; seeks understanding; helps those in need; self-doubt; creative imagination; considerate; kind; inspired; high aspirations **Water=Cups**

Please take note: In some decks, Coins replace the Pentacles, Rods replace the Wands, Vessels replace the Cups, and/or Sabers replace the Swords. I've always only referred to them as Coins, Wands, Cups, and Swords.

Nevertheless, no matter what is used, notice how particular *elements* share the same type of traits.

Not all of the Major Arcana cards have corresponding zodiac connections, but 17 out of the 22 do.

Aries ... The Fool

Libra and Taurus ... The Empress

Pisces... The Hierophant

Gemini... The Lovers

Leo... The Sun

Virgo and Sagittarius... The Hermit

Taurus... The Wheel of Fortune

Libra... Justice (of course, because of the scales)

Scorpio... Death

Aquarius... Temperance

Capricorn... The Devil

Aquarius... The Tower

Sagittarius... The Star

Cancer... The Moon

Leo... The Sun

Gemini... Judgment

Sagittarius... The World

PLANETS RULING HEALTH AND CORRESPONDING TAROT CARDS FOR THE CONNECTION

The SUN rules our physical body, eyes, blood circulation, high or low blood pressure, blood sugar, the heart, and the spinal system.

Connecting cards: The Sun and Strength are associated with Leo, which is ruled by the Sun.

The MOON rules the uterus, breasts, and the stomach.

Connecting card: The Moon is associated with Cancer, which is ruled by the Moon.

MERCURY rules nerves, lungs, shoulders, arms, hands, and cell structure.

Connecting cards: the Lovers, Judgment, and the Hermit.

Mercury rules two sun signs:

Gemini, represented by the Lovers and Judgment, rules the shoulders, arms, hands, and lungs.

Virgo, represented by the Hermit, rules the intestines, digestion, and the colon.

VENUS rules the throat, neck, kidneys, ovaries, and venous circulation.

Connecting cards: the Wheel of Fortune, Empress, and Justice

Venus rules two sun signs:

Taurus, represented by the Wheel of Fortune, rules the neck, throat, and venous circulation.

Libra, represented by the Empress, rules the ovaries, and Justice, rules the kidneys.

MARS rules red corpuscles, surgery, head, headaches, inflammations, reproduction, the intestines and the nose.

Connecting cards: The Fool and Death are both ruled by Mars.

Mars rules two sun signs:

Aries, represented by the Fool, rules the head, headaches, inflammations and red corpuscles.

Scorpio, represented by Death, rules the nose, surgery, and reproduction.

JUPITER rules the appetite, vision, hips, thighs, liver, arterial blood, cell growth, and accidents.

Connecting cards: The Star and the World are associated with Sagittarius, which is ruled by Jupiter.

SATURN rules skin, teeth, ears, knees, the skeleton, colds, rheumatism, arteries, and chronic illnesses.

Connecting card: The Devil is associated with Capricorn, which is ruled by Saturn.

URANUS rules calves, ankles, respiratory activity, spasms, abnormal growths, blood circulation or blood problems and accidents.

Connecting cards: The Tower and Temperance are associated with Aquarius, which is ruled by Uranus.

Aquarius, represented by the Tower, rules accidents, spasms, calves, ankles, and abnormal growths.

Aquarius, represented by Temperance, rules blood circulation, blood problems, and accidents.

NEPTUNE rules the feet, toes, alcohol, addictions, poison, mucous discharges, colds, and the pineal gland.

Connecting card: The Hierophant is associated with Pisces, which is ruled by Neptune.

THE SIMPLEST METHOD TO REMEMBER THE CONNECTIONS BETWEEN ASTROLOGICAL SIGNS AND PARTS OF THE BODY:

Aries... The head and inflammations

Taurus... The throat and neck

Gemini... The shoulders, arms, hands, and lungs

Cancer... The breasts, ovaries, uterus, and women's reproduction system

Leo... The heart and the eyes

Virgo... The colon, intestines, and digestion

Libra... The kidneys and the ovaries

Scorpio... Men's reproductive system, surgery, and sex!

Sagittarius... The hips and thighs

Capricorn... The knees, the ears, and rheumatism

Aquarius... The calves and ankles

Pisces... The feet, toes, and pineal gland

But you have to remember the cards that are associated with the sun signs!

THE TWELVE HOUSES

1st House... Your physical body and appearance, early environment, outward behavior, your personality and temperament, how the world sees you

2nd House... Finances, earning ability, possessions, money, materialistic goals

3rd House... Mind, communications, writing skills, messages, short journeys, perceptive abilities, mental aptitude, brothers, sisters, early education

4th House... Home, conditions toward end of life, parents, real estate holdings

5th House... Love life, relationships, dating, children, pleasures, speculations, high school

6th House... Job, health, attitudes towards both, service to others, small pets

7th House... Marriage, partnerships, lawsuits, contracts, open enemies

8th House... Other peoples' money, inheritance, insurance, taxes, investigators, rebirth, rehabilitation, surgery, death and everything concerning it, occult subjects, sex

9th House... Philosophy, religion, law, long trips, higher education

10th House... Career, profession, reputation, mother

11th House... Hopes, wishes, and dreams, friends, social activity

12th House... Sorrows, restrictions, unexpected difficulties, self-undoing, secret enemies, isolation, institutions, hospitalization, intuition, subconscious mind, large pets

I included the house definitions in case you want to do a "house reading." You could lay out 12 cards and connect them to each particular house.

For instance, if you had the Ace of Coins in the tenth position, it would definitely indicate a new job or promotion. If the Eight of Swords fell into the eighth position, that might indicate a problem with taxes or necessary surgery.

These are only suggestions... Remember, always see and say what you *feel!* Use your intuition and practice different methods.

Although I added layouts and interpretations, these are just examples. When reading someone, you are actually reading their *subconscious,* so I would most likely read the cards entirely different in that case. I would always tell the person that they already know what they want to know...they are just not *aware* of it since it's in their subconscious.

SYMBOLS FOUND IN TAROT CARDS

I've added this section in the updated version since this was in the notes from the class I attended in 1983. However, I've never delved into this extra information. Nevertheless, if you *really* want to get extraordinarily deep into the Tarot cards and study them obsessively (ha), you can actually get a bunch of additional "clues" if you follow these guidelines.

Example: If you are reading someone who wants to know if they are going to get a new boyfriend or a new job and in the cards you see a mountain, you will immediately know that there is some kind of obstacle that is holding the person back from attaining what she is hoping for. You could probably get that information from just looking at the Two of Swords (not seeing something that is in her way) or The Devil (something being hidden from her). Remember please that these two meanings are only how I would see it. No two readers interpret cards exactly the same!

I did not include these additional "clues" in the original publication but decided to in case some of my readers wanted to get deep into the cards!

Arm or Hands... Help

Armor... A guard or guardians

Astrological Symbol... The sign of the person it represents (of course)

Bat Wings... Drive you crazy

Beard... Wisdom

Bell... Message of love

Belt... Keep your pants up

Birds... Friends that help in fright or trouble

Boat... Trip but not necessarily by a boat

Bow Tie... Ties to someone

Bridge... Emotionally over something, passing over troubled waters

Butterfly... Pleasure

Capes... Protection or hiding something

Carrot... Someone cares

Cat... Warning of a change

Circle... Completion

Clouds... Attitude

Clown... Joker

Crescent Moon... Bad health (if facing down)

Crescent Moon... Intuition (if vertical)

Cross... Someone clever

Crutch... Help

Dogs... Friends or inheritance

Doll... Good to you

Dragon... Challenge

Elephant... Gift

Eye... Psychic

Feather... Finery

Fish... Sympathetic friend

Flower... Spending time with someone

Giraffe... Curiosity

Grapes... Abundance of sexuality

Halo, Glow... Person's mind and spirit

Hammer... Fool, any fool

Hat, Crown... Position

Heart... Emotions

Horn... Announcement

Horses (not white) or vehicles... A sometime boyfriend

Island... Time alone or feeling alone

Keyholes... Opportunity

Keys... Knowledge

Lamp... Wisdom

Lantern... Enlightenment

Leaves... Growth

Lilies... Spiritual

Lion... Courage and pride

Lizard... Annoyance

Mountain... Hidden obstacle

Octagon... Power structure

Peacock... Pride, value

Peak... Hope

Pears... Two-faced person

Petal... Joy

Pitchfork... Neptune (Neptune is ruled by Saturn
and represented by a pitchfork)

Rabbit... Much activity

Rain... Tears

Rainbow... Promises

Rings... Commitments

Roses... Love (color indicates the type of love)

Sand... Time

Scepter... Authority

Sky... Mood

Snake... Gossip

Snowman... Cold person

Socks... Protect yourself

Spider... Delay

Square... Foundation or difficulty

Star... Fame

Stem... Intensity

Sun... Happiness

Sunflower... Good happy times

Throne... Persons, places, or surroundings

Trees... Security

Triangle... Metaphysics

Turtle... Slowness

Volcano... Eruption

Water... Motion

White Horse... Job security

Wings... Protection

Wreath... Success

COLORS FOUND IN TAROT CARDS

An update to this book is the following list of colors that might help you gain a deeper understanding of the tarot cards. These were also in the notes from the class I attended in 1983. Again, I did not use the listed colors in my readings, at least not consciously. I do use colors when reading auras since I realized many years ago that I was able to see colors around others. This little talent really helps me stay away from certain people.

Red... Energy, excitement, power, aggression, danger, all things intense and passionate

Pink... Love, romance, caring, tenderness, and acceptance

Yellow... Intelligence and imagination, joy, happiness, friendship, optimism, jealousy, cowardice, deceit, and dishonesty

(Yellow has been associated with being a coward for a long time.)

Dark Blue... Integrity, knowledge, power, and sincerity

Blue... Peace, tranquility, harmony, security, order, confidence, trust, truth, and depression

Purple... Royalty, nobility, spirituality, wisdom, enlightenment, honor, cruelty and arrogance

Green... Growth, nature, renewal, good luck, fertility, vigor, jealousy, envy, and misfortune

Orange... Enthusiasm, warmth, vibrant, balance, expansive, flamboyant, demanding attention

Brown... Earthy, stability, reliability, simplicity, dishonesty, being untruthful

Beige and Ivory... Unifies pleasantness and simplicity if seen together

Gray... Modesty, dignity, maturity, old age, sorrow and boredom

White... Purity, protection, cleanliness, innocence, sterility, birth, youth, cold, and detached

Black... Elegance, wealth, mystery, sophistication, formality, remorse, sadness, mourning, and death (The color of the occult, which means "hidden")

Silver... Spending money, also a female card

Gold... Investing money, also a male card

Wow, doesn't the above two meanings scream of sexism? Spending money is connected to a female while investing money is related to a male.

THE GENERAL YEAR READING

This is a *general* year reading. Please keep this in mind. It is only for *general* guidance. As illustrated in the layout, Justice would be January. Then you would read the cards ***clockwise***. The Tower would represent February; the Eight of Pentacles would be March, the Ten of Pentacles would represent April, etc.

How would I read these cards? It would depend on the energy I felt from the querent. Please remember that no two readers interpret cards the same way. Nevertheless, here are a few clues, but note that I repeatedly say "could" in my explanations!

January: Justice could mean that the person is striving for more balance in his or her life. (Think New Year's resolutions.) Note that the card is *reversed*, which would indicate to me that it might be somewhat of a struggle or a slow start getting that balance in January.

February: The Tower could indicate that a completely unexpected event is going to happen.

March: The Eight of Pentacles could mean that the person is making more money than they have time to spend. On the other hand, it could mean that the person is working more than one job, making the money, but not having time to do anything BUT work!

April: The Ten of Pentacles indicates wealth...could be for the querent but also could mean a relationship with a wealthy person.

May: The King of Pentacles could indicate acquiring many possessions.

June: The Three of Wands could indicate a long distance journey.

July: The King of Swords could represent an interaction with an authority figure. Whoops! This might mean trouble since it could be a judge or a police officer.

August: The Four of Pentacles represent possibly purchasing a house or spending money on house expenses.

September: The Ace of Swords could represent a separation or complete severing of a relationship, which could be friendship or romantic. Since this card is *reversed*, the separation might be slow in coming during the month (will not happen quickly).

October: The Emperor could indicate that the querent should be careful in what he or she asks for since that is what he or she will get. (Be careful what you wish for...)

November: The Three of Pentacles could represent a marriage of money but could also indicate a lucrative partnership involving business endeavors.

December: The Two of Swords could indicate indecision and confusion and not seeing things correctly because the querent is blindfolded (figuratively).

Now that you get the general idea, you can experiment using this layout. You could even add two or three cards in the middle for a quick synopsis of the entire year. Just remember that this is *extremely* general.

THE CELTIC CROSS READING

The Celtic Cross is probably the most popular spread on the planet. Everyone with only a remote interest in Tarot cards seems to know about it.

The card in the center represents what's happening now. In this layout, it is the Five of Cups (under The Lovers), which could mean a disappointment in love. The Lovers card represents a challenge, and in this case it might indicate that the querent is still in love although disappointed in the current situation.

The Wheel of Fortune in the third position represents the distant past and could mean extremely good luck and extraordinary money.

However, the Nine of Pentacles in the fourth position represents the recent past and could mean that some of that great money was squandered away, possibly on a new car!

The fifth position is occupied by the Seven of Wands and indicates the outcome of the cards in positions three and four (distant past and recent past). This could mean success at the querent's job or with her work.

The card in the sixth position predicts the future, and, in this case, the Ace of Pentacles is good since it could mean more money in her hand, a raise in pay, a new job or an increase in her work to bring more money to the querent.

The four cards on the right are what I call the ultimate result. The seventh position is occupied by the Magician and can be interpreted as the querent. In this case, it might mean that she is in control of her own fate.

The card in the eighth position is the Eight of Cups. This position is called "external forces," but I see many times that it represents the subconscious, as in this case. The death of a love is still bothering her *subconsciously.*

The Sun is in the ninth position, which reveals the hopes and dreams of the querent. She desires happy times and pleasure in the simple life. Be careful here since The Sun can be a giver or a taker of life.

The final outcome is represented by the Eight of Wands, which indicates a balanced day's work and might disrupt her desire for a simple life. This person might be spending too much time doing too much work, or attempting to do more than she can handle.

I obviously "pretended" that the querent in this reading was a woman.

THE EXPANDED CELTIC CROSS
READING

This is an expanded version of the traditional Celtic Cross layout. You can obtain more information using this spread. It will also bring *changes* to the original Celtic Cross layout in this book.

The Fool is sitting on top of the center two cards, the Five of Cups and The Lovers. This could mean that the querent was being taken for a fool and now is starting a new journey away from the relationship.

The Page of Wands in the third position could indicate that the querent was wise in her work in the distant past. Remember, this adds meaning to the original card, the Wheel of Fortune, which indicated good money.

The Three of Cups in the fourth position might mean that she attended a party or a wedding in her recent past. Since the Nine of Pentacles was in the original position of the layout, it could mean that she drove to the party or wedding in her car.

The Page of Cups in the fifth position could mean that she is young-thinking, or maybe she is guilty of being a tad too childish while doing her work. Remember, this is the outcome of the cards in the third and fourth positions.

The Ten of Wands in the sixth position could mean a change of work or a change of plans. Since the Ace of Coins is already sitting there, it could possibly indicate more money in her hand because of a new job. Remember, this position predicts the future.

Now, let's look at the ultimate results cards on the right. Remember, the first card on the bottom, The Magician, signifies the querent. Right next to that card in the seventh position lays the Page of Coins. This unfortunately might mean only a small amount of money. From what I see so far in this reading, I feel that the querent might just have a spending problem. I would caution her at this point to work on managing her money more effectively.

The King of Wands sits in the eighth position next to the Eight of Cups. This would (or could) mean to me that important plans are coming her way. This would help her get over the death of a love, as indicated by the Eight of Cups.

The ninth position has the Six of Wands, which could mean that the querent will have peace of mind either in her work or in her home. This strengthens her hopes and dreams since the card joins the Sun, which signifies happy times and pleasure in the simple life.

The final outcome is represented by the Six of Cups, which could indicate many friends and a lot of company. This would help her relax since the

Eight of Cups might mean she is devoting too much time to work.

Again, I've obviously "pretended" that the querent was a woman.

THE PAST, PRESENT, FUTURE READING

This is a short and sweet reading where you lay out nine cards from left to right. Then you read them from *right to left*. The first three cards are your *past*. The next three cards are your *present*. The next three cards are your *future*

Although I have all the cards exposed, you might want to lay them out facing down, and then turn

72

three over at a time for the reading. Turn the cards over from top to bottom.

How would I interpret this layout? I would state that the past of the querent was very inhibited, and she felt trapped in a situation. A message was possibly received, and querent, in turn, followed that advice and ended the situation.

The next three cards represent the present and could possibly mean that money is coming in and going out at about the same rate. She might be busy making important plans or going after an important job. She could receive an offer but feels she can take it or leave it!

The final three cards show the querent has the strength to endure all the troubles of the past until it turns into joy. She has choices to make but finally realizes that her fate is in her hands. She will be in control. It will be like magic with many opportunities coming her way.

Please note that I again interpreted this reading "pretending" like the querent was a female.

THE FIVE CARD STORYTELLING READING

This is another short and sweet reading that will take only a minute or two to do. Lay the cards from left to right as shown although you might want to place them face down. Actually, that is your choice; either way is fine.

The Ten of Swords stands for the beginning of the story, or the present. This card might warn of an unjust treatment by a friend or a lover. Look at the picture...think backstabbing!

The Eight of Coins represents what leads to the middle and could indicate independence in a self-supporting business, or at least *wanting* a self-supporting business.

The Nine of Wands represents the middle and shows that the querent is only tolerating a situation regarding work and/or plans and is waiting for a change.

In the fourth position is the High Priestess and indicates that the querent has the self-knowledge to attain the end. This is the position that leads to the end.

The fifth position represents the end and the Ten of Wands in that position indicates a change of work and/or plans.

I particularly like this reading since you can quickly get a glimpse of what's going on in your life. Of course, you can use this layout when you are *doing* a reading for someone.

Made in United States
North Haven, CT
04 July 2024

54384295R00046